Easy
Patchwork
Jackets™

Edited by Jeanne Stauffer

HOUSE of
WHITE
BIRCHES

PUBLISHERS
SINCE 1947

Table of Contents

Abstract Jaket,
page 16

Strip Patchwork
in Black & White,
page 54

Denim & Floral Duo,
page 22

Flowers & Vines
Sweatshirt Jacket,
page 4

Welcome

Many quilters are proud of their quilting skills, and they should be. What better way is there to tell others that you love quilting than by creating a jacket? In *Easy Patchwork Jackets*, we share with you nine very unique jacket designs.

We have used a variety of techniques for these jackets. Two of the jackets are stitched using sweatshirts as the pattern: Flowers & Vines Sweatshirt Jacket and Abstract Jacket. The sweatshirt is the base for each one of them, but one applies patchwork and appliqué for an elegant look, and the other completely covers the sweatshirt with patchwork for a jacket that is extra warm.

For those quilters who like to use sewing patterns for wearables, we have included four jackets that use Kwik•Sew jacket pattern No. 3158. If you are a plus size, a similar pattern would be Kwik-Sew pattern No. 3585. Both patterns have dolman sleeves with cuffs that turn up. If you have a favorite jacket pattern already, read through the instructions for the jacket you want to make, and you may discover that you can use your pattern as well.

The Jelly Jacket uses 2½"-wide strips, and the Batik Beauty uses large fabric pieces. One of the jackets uses strip piecing in black and white for a more dramatic look. For a slightly heavier jacket, stitch our jacket made of denim.

Two of the jackets use patterns from designer Bren Bornyasz. She has her own unique style and a line of patterns. One of these jackets uses a different cutting technique to create a crazy quilt look. The second jacket is much longer, almost coat length, for those who prefer more coverage. As a bonus, we have included designs for two purses.

The last jacket we have selected for the book doesn't actually have any patchwork, but the trapunto technique used was so unique that we wanted to share it with you. It is also a jacket that says, "I am a quilter." For this jacket, you need to use fleece; other fabrics will not work. The sample was made using Kwik•Sew Pattern No. 3292, but other patterns would work also.

I know you are ready to make your first jacket; have fun doing so. These designs will tell the world that you are a quilter and that you love quilting. Make a jacket for every season and try every technique in this book. It is so satisfying to wear something your hands have stitched.

Happy quilting,

Jeanne Stauffer

Jeanne Stauffer

House of White Birches, Berne, Indiana 46711   DRGnetwork.com

Flowers & Vines Sweatshirt Jacket

By Lorine Mason

Use a sweatshirt as the base for this elegant appliquéd jacket.

Project Specifications
Skill Level: Beginner
Jacket Size: Size varies

Materials
- Ivory crewneck sweatshirt with inset sleeves
- ¼ yard green embroidered solid
- ¼ yard peach embroidered solid
- ½ yard blue/white pinstripe
- ½ yard large floral
- ½ yard green print
- Ivory all-purpose thread
- ¼ yard fusible web
- 5 yards ¼"-wide fusible web tape
- ⅞" yellow round button
- ⅝" green round button
- Water-erasable fabric marker
- Basic sewing tools and supplies

Cutting
1. Cut three 2" x 42" A strips from each fabric.

2. Cut 2"-wide bias strips from blue/white pinstripe to total 130".

3. Cut 1½"-wide bias strips from green print to total 175".

Preparing the Sweatshirt
1. Cut the sweatshirt apart, leaving the seams attached to the body of the sweatshirt along the neckline and sleeve openings as shown in Figure 1; cut the front down the center and around the front bottom corners, again referring to Figure 1.

Figure 1

2. Lay the sweatshirt right side up on top of a cutting mat with the left bottom edge of the shirt back over the 45-degree line and the right bottom corner of the sweatshirt at an intersection of a horizontal and vertical line on the mat as shown in Figure 2.

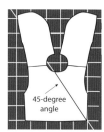

45-degree angle

Figure 2

3. Using a water-erasable fabric marker, mark the 45-degree line onto the sweatshirt, again referring to Figure 2.

4. Pin an A strip right side down, aligning the raw edge along the marked line as shown in Figure 3; sew through the fabric strip and the sweatshirt.

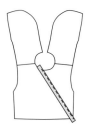

Figure 3

5. Fold the strip to the right side; press flat.

6. Place a second strip on top of the first strip with right sides together and raw edges even and pin; stitch through both layers of the fabric and sweatshirt. Press strip to the right side as shown in Figure 4. Continue adding strips, pinning, sewing and pressing each strip before proceeding to the next.

Note: Be sure to check the length of each strip before pinning by placing it right side up on the sweatshirt alongside the previous strip. This is important, as you will be surprised at how much length is required once the strip is turned to the right side.

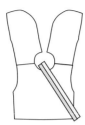

Figure 4

7. Stitch down the side edges of the sweatshirt to hold the strips in place.

8. Draw curved lines along the back and up over the shoulder to the left front of the sweatshirt. Continue the line across the right front of the sweatshirt as shown in Figure 5; repeat for the sleeves, starting at the center top and continuing down the length of the sleeve. Draw short stem lines referring to project photo and Placement Diagram for positioning.

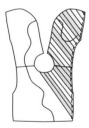

Figure 5

Completing the Appliqué

1. Join the 1½"-wide green print bias strips on short ends to make one long strip; press seams open.

2. Fold over ¼" and press each long edge of the bias strip; fold in half and press again to create bias for the stems.

3. Press the ¼"-wide fusible web tape to the wrong side of the pressed binding strip.

4. Starting at the bottom edge of the sweatshirt back, press the bias strip over the drawn lines starting with the short stems, cutting pieces to fit as you stitch. Finish with the vine, covering the ends of stems; press well. Stitch along both edges of the fused bias strips. Repeat on sleeves.

5. Cut the fusible web in half; press one half to the wrong side of the green floral; using the leaf pattern provided, trace 20 leaf shapes onto the paper side of the fused fabric. Cut out shapes on traced lines; remove paper backing.

6. Arrange and fuse the leaves on the sweatshirt back and sleeves along the stems and at the ends of each vine referring to the photo and Placement Diagram for positioning suggestions.

7. Select 11 flower motifs on the large floral print and cut fusible web shapes slightly larger than the motifs; bond the fusible web to the wrong side of the fabric behind the chosen shapes. Cut out motifs close to the edges of the designs; remove paper backing.

8. Arrange and fuse the motifs shapes at the ends of the stems.

9. Stitch around edges of each fused shape, through the centers of the leaf shapes and on some detail lines of the flower motifs to hold designs securely through washing and drying cycles. *Note: After laundering, fraying is to be expected and will only add to the design of the jacket.*

10. Pin the sleeves to the armholes and stitch using either a serger or sewing machine. *Note: If using a sewing machine, finish edges with an overcast stitch and press.*

11. Pin the sleeves and the front and back of the sweatshirt together along the side seams and stitch as in step 10.

Binding the Edges

1. Join the 2"-wide pinstripe bias strips on short ends to make one long binding strip; press seams open.

2. Fold under and press ¼" on one long edge of the strip.

3. Pin the raw edge of the binding strip right sides together with the raw edges of the front and bottom of the sweatshirt; stitch in place.

4. Turn the binding strip to the inside; hand-stitch in place. Press edges flat.

5. Turn under one end of the remaining binding strip ¼" and press. Pin the raw edge of the binding right sides together along the neckline of the sweatshirt, starting by aligning the pressed edge with the left front corner of the sweatshirt as shown in Figure 6; continue stitching all around the neckline.

Figure 6

6. Trim the binding, leaving a 5" section extending past the right side end; fold the extended raw edge and end under ¼" as shown in Figure 7.

Figure 7

7. Fold remainder of binding strip over the raw edge of the sweatshirt and hand-stitch in place. Machine-stitch along open edge and across end of the 5" extension as shown in Figure 8. Stitch across end.

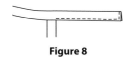

Figure 8

8. Fold the extended end down to make a loop and stitch in place on inside of sweatshirt to secure as shown in Figure 9.

Figure 9

9. Stitch the smaller button on top of the larger button and to the top edge of the sweatshirt jacket opposite the loop to finish. ❖

Flowers & Vines Sweatshirt Jacket Front
Placement Diagram
Size Varies

Flowers & Vines Sweatshirt Jacket Back
Placement Diagram

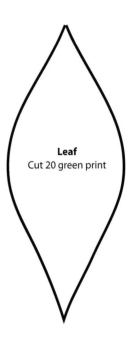

Leaf
Cut 20 green print

Stitch & Flip Jacket

By Bren Bornyasz

Red and black prints with gold-metallic accents combine to make a rich-looking patchwork jacket.

Project Notes

It is helpful to make a muslin test garment to make adjustments to the pattern before cutting the garment pieces. Change pattern as necessary.

This pattern is 4" longer than the commercial jacket pattern. You may make the jacket as long as desired by adding length to the bottom edge of your commercial jacket pattern.

Project Specifications

Skill Level: Intermediate
Jacket Size: Size varies

Materials

- ⅓ yard each 6 different red prints (some with gold-metallic accents)
- ⅓ yard each 6 different black prints (some with gold metallic accents)
- ½ yard black gold-metallic print for binding
- 3 yards lining fabric
- 3 yards interlining fabric
- All-purpose thread to match fabric
- Black pearl cotton
- Fabric pencil or marker
- Mount Fuji Jacket pattern from Brensan Studios
- 2 (6"-long) black Chinese frog closures
- Basic sewing tools and supplies

Cutting

1. Cut two 2¾" x 42" A strips from each of the 12 fabrics; subcut strips into 2¾" A squares.
2. Cut four 1¼" x 42" B strips from each of the 12 fabrics; set aside two strips each fabric. Subcut the remaining strips into 2¾" B rectangles.
3. Cut 2"-wide bias strips from binding fabric to total 120".

Completing Patchwork

1. Select one garment pattern piece from commercial pattern. Join A squares and B rectangles to make a strip longer than the garment pattern as shown in Figure 1, beginning and ending with A squares. Press seams in one direction. *Note: Ten or 12 A squares will fit most patterns.*

Figure 1

2. Continue piecing A-B strips until you have enough to cover the garment pattern.

3. Repeat with all pattern pieces.

Completing the Garment Sections

Note: Use a ¼" seam allowance for all steps in this section.

1. Cut the main pattern pieces from commercial jacket pattern from interlining fabric.

2. Mark the exact center of the back and sleeve pieces, drawing a line with a fabric marker or pencil.

3. Select one marked garment section. Center and pin an A-B strip down the marked centerline of the garment section, matching one A square with the bottom edge as shown in Figure 2.

4. Select an uncut B strip and audition along the edge of the first strip for color placement; when satisfied with your choice, pin the B strip right sides together with the A-B strip and stitch as shown in Figure 3. Press strip open.

5. Repeat steps 3 and 4 until the whole section is covered with strips.

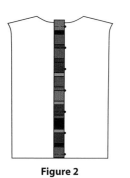
Figure 2

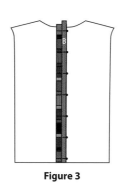
Figure 3

6. Trim edges of patchwork section even with the interlining piece as shown in Figure 4.

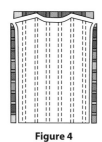
Figure 4

7. Repeat steps 3–6 for all garment sections, except align an A-B strip with the center edge of the jacket front interlining pieces as shown in Figure 5.

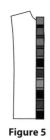
Figure 5

8. Add decorative stitching to garment sections as desired. *Note: The sample jacket shown was stitched in a meandering and curving pattern from top to bottom from the interlining side along patchwork strips using black pearl cotton.*

Completing the Jacket
Note: Use a ½" seam allowance for all steps in this section.

1. Cut front and back lining pieces using patchwork pieces for patterns. Cut sleeve-lining pieces using commercial pattern.

2. To complete jacket shell, with right sides together, sew jacket front pieces to jacket back at shoulder seams; add sleeves. Stitch side seams from bottom edge of front/back to edge of sleeve. Press seams open.

3. Complete jacket lining as for jacket shell; press seams open.

4. Insert lining inside jacket, wrong sides together, matching seams and edges; press layers flat and baste together.

5. Cut cuff pieces and complete the sleeves referring to commercial pattern.

6. Join the binding strips on short ends to make one long strip as shown in Figure 6; trim seams to ¼" and press seams open.

Figure 6

7. Pin binding strip right sides together with the jacket with raw edges even; stitch all around, mitering corners and overlapping at the beginning and end.

8. Press binding strip to the wrong side, turn under raw edge ¼" and hand-stitch binding in place.

9. Sew frog closures to the jacket front in desired locations to finish. ❖

Stitch & Flip Jacket Front
Placement Diagram
Size Varies

Stitch & Flip Jacket Back
Placement Diagram
Size Varies

Abstract Jacket

By Colleen Granger

Using a sweatshirt as a base, this patchwork jacket is both warm and comfortable.

Project Specifications
Skill Level: Intermediate
Jacket Size: Size varies

Materials
- 12 fat quarters or ¼ yard of 12 fabrics
- 1½ yards black solid
- Black crewneck sweatshirt with set-in sleeves at least one size larger than normal to allow for losing 1" on each side
- Neutral-color all-purpose thread
- Black 22" separating sports zipper
- Fabric marking tool visible on black
- Fabric spray adhesive
- Basic sewing tools and supplies

Preparing the Sweatshirt

1. Remove lower ribbing from the sweatshirt.

2. Lay the trimmed sweatshirt out on a flat surface with the front facing up; smooth out shirt, making sure it is not distorted.

3. Use a tape measure or cutting ruler to measure between top of sleeve seams to find center point in jacket front, mark point. Move tape down to just under the sleeves and measure again from side to side; find center point and mark it.

4. Move tape down again to a couple of inches from the lower edge; find and mark the center point.

5. Use a cutting ruler to align three center points, draw a line down the center of the shirt. *Note: Do not use powdered chalk to mark line, as it will disappear during the construction process; use hard chalk or other suitable marker.*

6. Mark an X at one underarm point and on the corresponding sleeve. Mark an O at the other underarm point and corresponding sleeve. *Note: These marks are used during the assembly process.*

7. Carefully cut up each side of sweatshirt to underarm point. If your sweatshirt has side seams, remove seams by cutting close to the seams. Turn sweatshirt fuzzy side out.

8. Cut as close as possible along the seam that attaches the sleeve to the body of the sweatshirt; remove the sleeve. Remove the seam and discard; repeat for other sleeve.

9. Remove underarm seam from each sleeve and remove cuff (ribbing); sleeves should now lie flat.

10. Remove the shoulder seams by cutting on each side of seam, cut through ribbing but do not remove neck ribbing. *Note: You will not cut up the front of the sweatshirt until the end.*

11. With a tape measure or ruler, measure sweatshirt pieces at the widest points and write down the following measurements:

Width of shirt front _____

Width of sleeve _____

Length of shirt front _____

Length of sleeve _____

Cutting

1. Cut fat quarters or ¼-yard pieces in half to make rectangles approximately 9" x 21"; divide the rectangles into two stacks.

2. Cut one stack of rectangles into 1", 1½", 1¾", 2" and 2½"-wide by 21"-long strips for the jacket body; place in a bag and mix. ***Note:*** *It is fine if strips are wider at one end than the other; this will enhance the design.*

3. Cut the remaining rectangles into 1", 1¼", 1½", 1¾" and 2"-wide by 21"-long strips for sleeves; place in a bag and mix.

4. Lay the black solid on a flat surface; cut two 42"-long strips 4" wide at one end and 2" wide at the other end to make A accent strips for jacket body as shown in Figure 1.

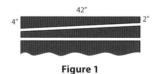

Figure 1

5. From black solid, cut four 36"-long strips 1½" wide at one end and 3" at the other end to make B accent strips for sleeves as shown in Figure 2.

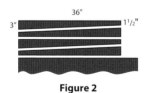

Figure 2

6. Cut four pocket pieces from black solid using pattern given.

7. Cut 150" of 3"-wide bias strips from black solid for binding.

Making the Body Fabric

1. Using the bag of strips cut for the jacket body, randomly select two strips and sew them together along 21" length using a ¼" seam allowance.

Continue sewing strips together in pairs until you have used them all; press all seams open.

2. Place stitched strips back in the bag and mix again; select two stitched strips and sew together as in step 1. Repeat until you have used all the strips; press seams open.

3. Continue to join in this manner until you have one unit 3"–4" wider than the width of the shirt front; trim ragged edges even as shown in Figure 3.

Figure 3

4. Repeat to sew remaining strip pairs to make two units at least 20" wide; trim ragged edges.

5. Cut the piece made in step 3 in half on one diagonal, slightly offsetting the cut as shown in Figure 4. ***Note:*** *Placement of ruler is not at corners. Half of the piece is used for the front of the jacket and the other for the back.*

Figure 4

6. Cut the 20" units as in step 5.

7. Lay out and join the body pieces with the largest section on the bottom, then an A jacket accent strip and one of each of the two smaller sections above as shown in Figure 5 to make jacket front section; press seams toward A strip. Repeat to make jacket back section.

Figure 5

Making Sleeve Fabric

1. Using the bag of strips cut for the sleeve, join as for jacket body to make one 21" x 24" rectangle and two 21" x 18" rectangles; trim ragged edges.

2. Cut stripped rectangles diagonally, cutting the larger rectangle from the upper right to lower left and the smaller rectangles from the upper left to the lower right as shown in Figure 6.

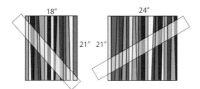

Figure 6

3. Lay out and join one of each sleeve section with two sleeve B accent strips to make one sleeve B section as shown in Figure 7; press seams toward B strips. Repeat to make two sleeve sections.

Figure 7

Attaching Fabric to Sweatshirt Pieces

1. Lay one pieced body section wrong side up on a flat surface.

2. Using a washable spray adhesive, spray fuzzy side of sweatshirt.

3. Carefully turn the sweatshirt piece with fuzzy side onto the wrong side of the pieced body section, aligning sweatshirt piece with the accent strip in the location you want as shown in Figure 8; gently press sweatshirt to fabric with hands, being careful not to distort or stretch.

Figure 8

4. Trim away excess fabric around sweatshirt body.

5. Repeat steps 1–4 to complete two each body and sleeve pieces.

6. Machine-quilt each section as desired. ***Note:*** *Using a machine decorative stitch along seam lines with matching or contrasting thread helps hold layers together.*

7. When quilting is complete, using a small zigzag stitch and starting at the neckband, stitch around the outer edge of the body section to hold strip ends in place; repeat for second body section. Repeat around the edges of each sleeve.

Jacket Assembly

1. Pin and stitch one pocket piece to the left and right side of the front body section as shown in Figure 9; repeat on the back section. Press pocket away from each body section.

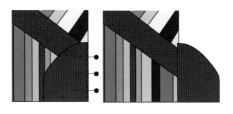

Figure 9

2. With right sides of the body sections together, join at shoulder seams; press seams open.

3. Match and pin the marked X on one sleeve with the X on the body section with right sides together. Pin the other underarm point of sleeve with underarm point of body section; fold piece in half, matching pins. Bring pieces together at the fold and pin. Continue folding and pinning until the sleeve is pinned in place; sew to attach sleeve. Repeat for the O sleeve.

4. Fold jacket in half with right sides together.

5. Pin along lower edge of sleeve, match sleeve seam, then down side and around pocket. Sew seams; repeat for other side. *Note: See pocket pattern for side-seam sewing mark for lower edge of pocket.*

6. Press pockets to the front of the jacket; fold raw edges in along seam line and whipstitch to lining.

7. Cut along the marked centerline on front of sweatshirt with shears.

8. Turn jacket right side out; try on. Mark sleeve length and trim neckline as needed; do not remove the seam line that attached the bottom ribbing to the body of the sweatshirt, this is needed for stability.

9. Join the 3"-wide bias strips on short ends to make one long strip as shown in Figure 10; press seams open.

Figure 10

10. Fold the binding strip in half with wrong sides together along length; press.

11. Place binding right sides together on the right side of jacket, matching raw edges of binding with raw edges of jacket, stitch all around outer edges of jacket and sleeves, overlapping at the beginning and end. Press binding away from jacket; hand-stitch in place on the inside of the jacket to complete binding.

12. Sew a separating sport zipper at the center front referring to zipper insertion instructions to finish. ❖

Abstract Jacket Front
Placement Diagram
Size Varies

Abstract Jacket Back
Placement Diagram
Size Varies

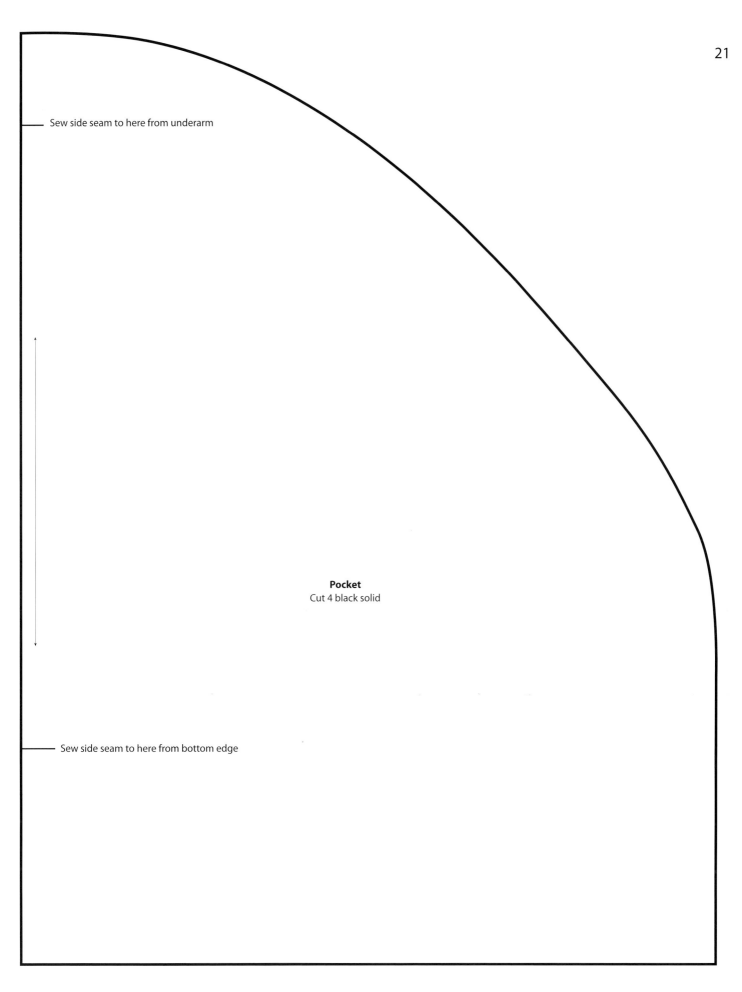

Sew side seam to here from underarm

Pocket
Cut 4 black solid

Sew side seam to here from bottom edge

House of White Birches, Berne, Indiana 46711   DRGnetwork.com

Denim & Floral Duo

By Chris Malone

Make a jazzy denim jacket and matching tote for almost any occasion.

Project Note

The sample jacket was made with Kwik•Sew pattern No. 3158 View A without batting.

Materials

- Scraps assorted blue prints, tonals and florals
- ⅛ yard red dot
- ⅛ yard gold print
- ¼ yard medium blue tonal
- ½ yard green print
- ⅔ yard royal blue print
- 1½ yards cream/blue print
- 1½ yards 60"-wide blue denim
- 2½ yards dark blue tonal
- ¾ yard fusible fleece
- ⅜ yard thin batting
- Neutral-color all-purpose thread
- Thread to match appliqué fabrics
- Kwik•Sew 3158 pattern
- ⅛ yard fusible interfacing
- 13 (1⅛") cover buttons
- 2⅞" x 13⅞" rectangle plastic needlepoint canvas or heavyweight cardboard
- No-fray solution
- Basic sewing tools and supplies

Cutting

1. Cut (35) 2½" x 2½" A squares assorted blue scraps.

2. Cut seven 2⅞" x 2⅞" D squares assorted blue scraps.

3. Cut (20–25) 1½"–3" x 14½" F strips assorted blue scraps.

4. Cut two 1¾" x 14½" G strips assorted blue scraps.

5. Cut one 2½" x 42" strip red dot; subcut strip into five 2½" squares for covered buttons.

6. Cut one 2⅞" x 42" strip medium blue tonal; subcut strip into seven 2⅞" E squares and four 2½" x 2½" squares for covered buttons.

7. Cut one 2½" x 14½" H strip medium blue tonal.

8. Cut two 1¼" x 22" bias strips green print for vines.

9. Cut one 11½" x 42" strip royal blue print; subcut strip into two 14½" rectangles for tote lining.

10. Cut one 3½" x 37" strip royal blue print for tote gusset lining.

11. Cut two 2" x 23" strips royal blue print for tote handle linings.

12. Cut one 3½" x 37" K strip blue denim.

13. Cut one 11½" x 14½" L piece blue denim.

14. Cut two 2" x 23" N pieces blue denim.

15. Cut jacket sleeves, side panels, collar and pocket from blue denim using commercial pattern.

16. Cut two 1½" x 28½" B strips cream/blue print.

17. Cut one 1½" x 14½" I strip cream/blue print.

18. Cut two 4½" x 8½" M rectangles cream/blue print.

19. Cut jacket sleeve lining pieces from cream/blue print using commercial pattern.

20. Cut two 6½" x 28½" C strips dark blue tonal.

21. Cut one 2" x 42" strip dark blue tonal for tote binding.

22. Cut one 3¾" x 42" strip dark blue tonal; subcut one 14½" J strip and four 2½" x 2½" squares for covered buttons.

23. Cut jacket front, back and collar lining pieces from dark blue tonal using commercial pattern.

24. Cut jacket edge and pocket binding from dark blue tonal using commercial pattern.

25. Cut one piece each 4" x 25" and 4" x 20" thin batting.

Jacket

Project Specifications

Skill Level: Intermediate
Jacket Size: Size varies

Completing the Patchwork

Note: All seams are ¼" and stitched with right sides together unless otherwise directed.

1. Prepare a tissue-paper pattern for the front and back pieces in the desired jacket size.

2. Join 14 A squares to make a strip; press seams in one direction.

3. Sew a B and C strip to opposite long sides of the A strip to complete the pieced back panel as shown in Figure 1; press seams toward B and C strips.

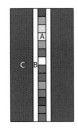

Figure 1

4. Fold the pieced back panel down the center; center the tissue-paper back pattern on the folded back panel as shown in Figure 2 and cut out; set aside.

Figure 2

5. Draw a diagonal line from corner to corner on the wrong side of each D square.

6. Place a D square right sides together with an E square; stitch ¼" on each side of the marked line as shown in Figure 3. Cut apart on the marked line and press D to the right side to complete two D-E units, again referring to Figure 3. Repeat to make 14 D-E units.

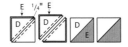

Figure 3

7. Divide the D-E units into two groups of seven each. Join one group of seven to make a 2½" x 14½"

D-E strip as shown in Figure 4; press seams in one direction. Repeat to make two D-E strips.

Figure 4

8. Join seven A squares to make an A strip; press seams in one direction. Repeat to make two A strips.

9. Draw a 45-degree-angle line from the center front to the outside edge of one tissue-paper front panel as shown in Figure 5; repeat on the opposite front panel, again referring to Figure 5.

Figure 5

10. Pin an F strip right side up on one tissue-paper pattern, aligning one long edge with the traced line as shown in Figure 6; place a second F strip right sides together with the pinned strip and stitch a ¼" seam. Press the second F strip to the right side.

Figure 6

11. Continue adding F strips and one each A and D-E strips as desired to cover the entire tissue paper referring to the project photo and Placement Diagram for suggested positioning of A and D-E strips; trim to paper edges to complete one front panel. Repeat to complete the second front panel; remove paper pattern.

Completing the Jacket Shell

Note: Use a ½" seam allowance for all steps in this section.

1. Complete the jacket shell referring to the commercial pattern.

2. Prepare one lined and bound pocket referring to the commercial pattern. Set aside pocket until appliqué pieces are prepared.

6. Sew all around on traced lines; cut out ⅛" from seam. Trim batting close to stitches.

7. Make a slash through one layer only of fabric; apply no-fray solution to cut edges and let dry.

8. Turn leaves right side out through the slashes; press. Whipstitch slashed edges together; machine topstitch through the center of each leaf with matching thread. Set aside four leaves for tote.

9. Repeat steps 5–9 using the 4" x 20" batting piece to make five flowers from gold print; topstitch ¼" from the edge all around each flower using thread to match fabric. Set aside two flowers for tote.

10. Position two leaves at each end of the vine; attach in place by stitching through the center of each leaf with thread to match fabric as shown in Figure 8.

Figure 8

Adding Appliqué Motifs

1. Fold one green print bias strip in half with wrong sides together along the length; stitch a ¼" seam along the long edge.

2. Trim the seam to a scant ⅛"; refold the strip, centering the stitched seam on the back as shown in Figure 7 to complete vine piece.

Figure 7

3. Fold a ¼" hem at one end of the vine piece; pin to jacket back near left shoulder. Arrange and pin the vine across the back in a gentle curve and over the right shoulder, ending on the upper right front patchwork in the "corsage" position referring to the Placement Diagram. Trim any excess; turn under a ¼" seam at the trimmed end.

4. Hand-stitch the vine in place using thread to match the fabric.

5. Trace leaf pattern 10 times on the wrong side of the green print. Fold the fabric in half with right sides together with traced leaves on top; pin to the 4" x 25" batting piece.

11. Refer to instructions with cover buttons to prepare five red dot covered buttons; set aside two for tote.

12. Position and pin a flower at each end of the vine, covering one end of the leaves; place a red covered button in the center of each flower and stitch in place stitching flower and button in place at the same time.

13. Place two leaves and one flower on the prepared pocket piece; stitch in place as in steps 10 and 12.

Completing the Jacket

1. Pin the completed pocket on the left jacket front 1" from bottom edge and 3½" from center front edge; machine-stitch in place around outside edge of binding.

2. Prepare jacket lining using the commercial pattern and instructions.

3. Follow pattern instructions to construct jacket with lining, finish button loops and bind jacket edges.

4. Refer to instructions with cover button to prepare four medium blue tonal covered buttons. Stitch a button to the opposite front edge to correspond to the placement of the button loops.

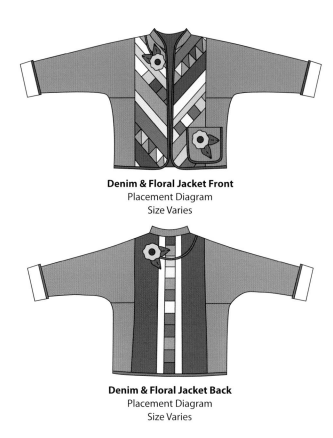

Denim & Floral Jacket Front
Placement Diagram
Size Varies

Denim & Floral Jacket Back
Placement Diagram
Size Varies

Denim Tote

Project Specifications
Skill Level: Intermediate
Tote Size: 14" x 11" x 3"

Instructions
1. Join seven A squares to make an A strip; press seams in one direction.

2. Arrange and join the A strip with G–J strips as shown in Figure 9; press seams in one direction.

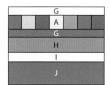

Figure 9

3. Prepare the remaining length of green print bias vine referring to Adding Appliqué Motifs for jacket.

4. Cut the vine piece into one each 9½" and 4½" lengths.

5. Turn under ¼" on one end of the vine pieces; arrange the vine pieces, leaves and flowers on the patchwork piece referring to Figure 10; stitch in place as for jacket to complete the tote front.

Figure 10

6. Bond fusible fleece to the wrong side of the tote front, L back and K gusset strip.

7. Stitch one long side of the K gusset strip down one side, across the bottom and up the other side of the tote front as shown in Figure 11, pivoting with the needle down at each corner; trim gusset ends even with tote front, if necessary. Clip corners close to stitching.

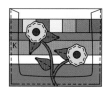

Figure 11

8. Stitch the other long edge of the K gusset piece to the side, bottom and side of the L back piece as in step 7; press both seam allowances and turn right side out.

9. To make the inside pocket, pin the two M rectangles right sides together and sew all around, leaving a 3" opening along one edge. Clip corners; turn right side out. Fold in seam allowance; whipstitch the opening closed and press.

10. Topstitch ¼" from the edge on sides and bottom of pocket; pin to the right side of one lining rectangle, centered 2½" down from top edge. Sew in place close to pocket edge on sides and bottom. Sew an additional line down the pocket center to divide it into two pockets as shown in Figure 12.

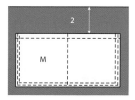

Figure 12

11. Join lining front, back and gusset pieces as in steps 7 and 8; do not turn right side out.

12. Place the plastic canvas or cardboard rectangle in the bottom of the stitched tote shell; insert the lining into the top shell, matching side seams. Stitch together around the top edge with a ³⁄₁₆" seam allowance.

13. Fold the dark blue tonal binding strip in half with wrong sides together along length; press.

14. Sew binding to the inside top edge of the tote, starting at the back and overlapping the ends. Press the binding strip flat; fold to the right side of the tote and topstitch close to the edge through all layers to finish the top of the tote.

15. Pin an N handle strip to a lining strip with right sides together; sew all around leaving a 3" opening on one side. Clip corners; turn right side out. Fold in seam allowance at opening; press and whipstitch opening closed. Topstitch ¼" from edge all around. Repeat to make two handles.

16. Prepare four dark blue tonal covered buttons referring to manufacturer's instructions.

17. Arrange both ends of one handle on tote front 2¼" in from side seams and 1½" down from top edge as shown in Figure 13; repeat on tote back.

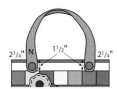

Figure 13

18. Sew a few small stitches through the handles and tote and then add a button to each end of each handle and stitch again to secure. ❖

Denim & Floral Bag
Placement Diagram 14" x 11" x 3"

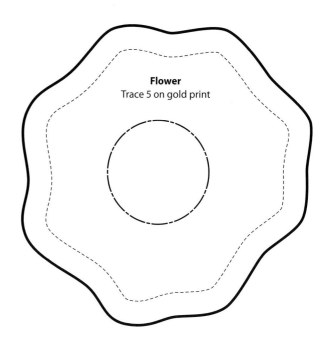

Flower
Trace 5 on gold print

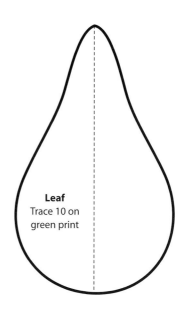

Leaf
Trace 10 on
green print

House of White Birches, Berne, Indiana 46711   DRGnetwork.com

Stack & Cut Squares Jacket

By Bren Bornyasz

Make a scrappy-but-elegant jacket in autumn colors.

Project Notes
It is helpful to make a muslin test garment to make adjustments to the pattern before cutting the garment pieces. Change pattern as necessary. Embellish the finished jacket with couched threads, buttons or beads.

Project Specifications
Skill Level: Beginner
Jacket Size: Size varies
Block Size: 2½" x 2½"
Number of Blocks: Varies depending on jacket size

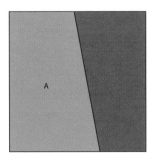

Stack & Cut Square
2½" x 2½" Block
Make 350 for small/medium size
Make 400 for large/extra-large size

Materials
- Autumn-colored scraps
- 1½ yards brown dot
- 2½ yards muslin
- Lining as per pattern for chosen size
- All-purpose thread to match fabrics
- Pearl rayon thread (optional)
- 1 yard interfacing
- Fabric pencil or marker
- The Quarter Circle Jacket BSS111 pattern from Brensan Studios
- Basic sewing tools and supplies

Cutting
1. Cut two 4" by fabric width strips brown dot; subcut into (14) 4" A squares.

2. Cut one 2" by fabric width strip brown dot; subcut into one 14" strip for button loops and one 28" binding strip.

3. Cut collar and facing pieces from brown dot.

4. From autumn-colored scraps, cut (350) 4" x 4" A squares for small/medium or 400 for large/extra large.

5. Cut the jacket pieces from muslin, lining and interfacing referring to purchased pattern.

Completing the Blocks
1. Stack A squares, selecting as many as you can comfortably cut using your rotary cutter.

2. Starting in the center of one side, cut a diagonal line from the center to about 1¼" from the corner on the opposite end as shown in Figure 1; stack like pieces together. **Note:** *The cuts do not need to be exact because after stitching they are trimmed to size.*

2"

1¼"

Figure 1

3. Repeat steps 1 and 2 until all A squares have been cut.

4. Select a different fabric piece from each stack; stitch together using a ¼" seam allowance to make an A unit as shown in Figure 2; repeat with all pieces. Press seams in one direction.

Figure 2

5. Stack several squares together and trim to 3" square to complete the blocks as shown in Figure 3.

Figure 3

Completing the Jacket Pieces

Note: Use a ¼" seam allowance for all steps in this section.

1. Using the muslin pieces, mark the exact center along the length of each garment section by drawing a line using a fabric pencil or marker. *Note: Sometimes the straight-of-grain lines on the pattern are in the center of the sleeve piece.*

2. Arrange and join Stack & Cut Square blocks to make an A strip that will fit along the length of the longest pattern piece as shown in Figure 4; press seams in one direction. Repeat to make additional strips until all units have been used.

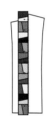

Figure 4   **Figure 5**

3. Select one garment section—sleeve, front or back. Center and pin an A strip down the marked centerline of the garment section as shown in Figure 5.

4. Select a second A strip and audition with the first strip for color placement; when satisfied with your choice, pin the second strip right sides together with the first strip and stitch a ¼" seam as shown in Figure 6. Press strip open.

Figure 6

5. Repeat step 5 until the whole section is covered with strips.

6. Quilt each section as desired by hand or machine. *Note: The sample jacket uses a pearl rayon thread in the bobbin to stitch long meandering lines from the back side of each piece.*

7. Trim edges of patchwork section even with the muslin piece as shown in Figure 7.

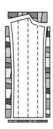

Figure 7

8. Repeat steps 5 and 6 for all garment sections.

9. Fold the button loop strip in half along the length; press to crease the centerline as shown in Figure 8. Open out strip and fold each side to the centerline on the wrong side; press.

Figure 8

10. Fold again on the centerline; press. Topstitch along each long side as shown in Figure 9.

Figure 9

11. Cut the stitched button loop strip into four 3½" lengths.

12. Select one button loop strip; fold each end over and down at an angle from the center of the strip as shown in Figure 10; press to hold. Repeat for all button loop strips.

Figure 10

13. Measure and mark 4½" from top inside edge of the pieced right front section for first loop placement; measure 4" from the marked line and mark for second loop. Repeat to mark for a total of four loops.

14. Position and pin one end of one loop with folded side against the right side of the right front section as shown in Figure 11; repeat for second end of loop and all other loops. Machine-baste ends in place, again referring to Figure 11.

Figure 11

Completing the Jacket

Note: Use a ½" seam allowance for all steps in this section.

1. Construct jacket following instructions given with the commercial pattern.

2. Baste raw edges of sleeve lining and outer sleeve together to create excess lining for ease of movement when wearing the jacket.

3. Mark button positioning on left front piece using loops as a guide; stitch buttons in place.

4. Measure the distance around the bottom edge of one sleeve; add 1" and cut two strips this length from binding. Join the ends of one binding strip to make a tube as shown in Figure 12; press seam open. Repeat for second binding strip.

Figure 12

5. Press under one long edge of the tube ½" as shown in Figure 13.

Figure 13

6. With right sides together and raw edges of lining, jacket and binding even, stitch all around sleeve opening using a ½" seam allowance; press the binding down and to the inside of the sleeve; hand-stitch in place to finish. Repeat for second sleeve. ❖

Stack & Cut Squares Jacket Front
Placement Diagram
Size Varies

Stack & Cut Squares Jacket Back
Placement Diagram
Size Varies

House of White Birches, Berne, Indiana 46711   DRGnetwork.com

Feathered Fleece Jacket

By Connie Kauffman

Fleece makes a soft, attractive jacket, and it's easy to give the quilting a trapunto or raised look.

Project Specifications

Skill Level: Beginner
Jacket Size: Size varies

Materials

- Kwik•Sew pattern 3292
- Fleece—add ½ yard to the fabric requirements for your size on the purchased pattern view B for jacket body
- Stabilizer (optional)
- All-purpose thread slightly darker than the fleece
- Temporary spray adhesive
- Tissue paper
- 1 yard fusible interfacing
- Basic sewing tools and supplies

Cutting

1. Cut jacket pieces using commercial pattern.

2. Cut a 13" x 13" square of fleece, cutting so that the fabric stretches in the opposite direction as the jacket back, as shown in Figure 1.

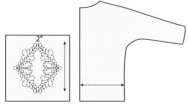

Figure 1

3. Cut two 8" x 20" strips of fleece for lapel quilting designs.

Jacket Construction

Note: When sewing with fleece fabric, it is helpful to use your machine's walking foot for sewing all seams using a slightly longer stitch length to keep fabric feeding through the machine smoothly.

1. Refer to numbered instructions with pattern to construct jacket with the following additions.

2. Sew back seam with a straight stitch; press seam open.

3. Transfer back quilting design to tissue paper, referring to the complete back design drawing to trace second half of design; cut out leaving a few inches of paper outside the design.

4. Lightly spray the back side of the tissue-paper pattern with temporary spray adhesive.

5. Position the sprayed design about 6" below the neckline edge on the right side of the seamed jacket back, aligning the center of the design with the center-back seam.

6. Lightly spray the right side of the matching-size piece of fleece with temporary spray adhesive.

7. Place the sprayed fleece against the wrong side of the jacket back behind the placed tissue design and finger-press in place. ***Note:*** *Check to be sure that the sprayed fleece piece stretches in the opposite direction as the jacket back fabric and that all areas of the paper design have the piece of fleece behind them; there will be three layers to stitch through. It is difficult to tell the right and wrong side of some fleece. If this is the case, there is no need to worry about right and wrong sides.*

8. Using matching all-purpose thread in the top of the machine and an open-toe quilting foot, sew over the lines on the tissue paper.

9. Using sharp scissors, cut off excess fleece from around the outside edge and in the open center of the fleece piece on the inside of the jacket as shown in Figure 2, being careful not to clip through the jacket back.

Figure 2

10. Trace the lapel quilting design onto two pieces of tissue paper, reversing one pattern.

11. Lightly spray the back side of the tissue-paper pattern with temporary spray adhesive.

12. Lightly spray temporary adhesive to the matching-size fleece pieces.

13. Stitch and trim as for back referring to steps 8 and 9 and Figure 3 for direction of stitching on feather designs.

Figure 3

14. Fuse interfacing to the wrong side of each stitched front facing piece.

15. Continue jacket construction referring to pattern instructions, stitching in the ditch along the back of the collar seam as shown in Figure 4.

Figure 4

16. Sew over sections of the stitched feather design on jacket lapel to hold the lapel layers together when wearing as shown in red in Figure 5 for stitching suggestions. **Note:** *Some parts of the feathers will be sewn over, but if sewn carefully seams will blend into the fleece and are not visible.*

Figure 5

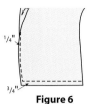

Figure 6

17. Topstitch jacket front ¼" from edge beginning at the bottom of feathers to the bottom edge of jacket as shown in Figure 6; stitch ¾" from bottom edge and at ends of sleeves. ❖

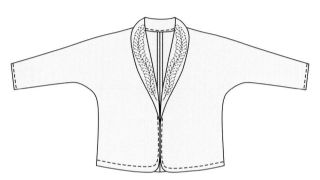

Feathered Fleece Jacket Front
Placement Diagram
Size Varies

Feathered Fleece Jacket Back
Placement Diagram
Size Varies

A Match on line to make complete pattern B

Lapel Quilting Design

A Match on line to make complete pattern B

Center

$^1/_2$ **Back Quilting Design**

Jelly Jacket & Purse

By Connie Kauffman

Jelly Roll strips in pastel florals combine to make a pretty summertime jacket with matching purse.

Project Notes
The sample jacket was made with Kwik•Sew pattern No. 3158 View B without batting to make a lightweight summer jacket. The matching purse makes this an elegant ensemble.

Materials
- Moda Jelly Roll™ of soft-colored floral strips or (25) 2½" x 42" strips
- ½ yard yellow floral
- ¾ yard blue floral
- 2 yards green large floral
- 3 yards cream floral
- ½ yard fusible fleece
- Neutral color all-purpose thread
- Variegated thread to match fabrics
- Kwik•Sew 3158 pattern
- 10 (¼") cream round buttons
- ¾" cream round shank button
- 4" (⅛"-wide) cream satin ribbon
- Tissue paper
- Basic sewing tools and supplies

Cutting
1. Cut one 13½" x 25½" D piece yellow floral for purse lining and top strip.

2. Cut four jacket side pieces blue floral using commercial pattern.

3. Cut two 9½" x 13½" E pieces blue floral for purse inner pockets.

4. Cut jacket sleeves and view B collar pieces from green large floral using commercial pattern.

5. Cut one 8" x 13½" A piece green large floral for purse bottom.

6. Cut jacket lining from cream floral using commercial pattern.

7. From Jelly Roll/2½" strips, cut the following: two 13½" B pieces from cream strip (purse sides); two 13½" C pieces from green strip (purse); (10) 2½"

F squares total from two or three different-color strips (prairie points); two 21" G pieces from yellow strip (handles); and two 7" H pieces from pink strip (purse flap).

8. From fusible fleece, cut the following: one 13½" x 19½" purse body piece; two ¾" x 20" handle pieces; and one 2" x 6¼" flap piece.

Jelly Jacket

Project Specifications
Skill Level: Intermediate
Jacket Size: Size varies

Completing the Patchwork
Note: Use a ¼" seam allowance for steps in this section.

1. Prepare tissue-paper patterns for the back and right and left front pieces using the commercial pattern.

2. Lay out the 2½" strips on the tissue-paper back piece in a pleasing arrangement from top to bottom; remove paper pattern without disturbing the order of the strips.

3. Starting at the bottom of the tissue-paper pattern, pin the first strip right side up on the tissue-paper pattern, aligning bottom edges; trim strip, leaving some excess beyond the pattern as shown in Figure 1.

Figure 1

4. Place the next strip right sides together with the first strip; trim as in step 3. Stitch along matching top edges to attach to paper as shown in Figure 2; press the top piece to the right side.

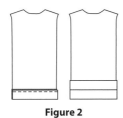

Figure 2

5. Repeat step 4 until the tissue-paper pattern is covered with strips.

6. Turn tissue-paper pattern over and trim excess fabric all around; remove tissue-paper pattern.

7. Repeat steps 3–6 to complete the two front panels, keeping the same fabric order as on the back.

Completing the Jacket
Note: Use a ½" seam allowance for all steps in this section.

1. Complete the jacket referring to the commercial pattern instructions.

2. Stitch in the ditch along some of the seams on the back panel to hold the lining and jacket outside pieces together.

3. Topstitch ¼" from edges around the cuff, collar and front edges using variegated thread to finish.

Jelly Jacket Front
Placement Diagram
Size Varies

Jelly Jacket Back
Placement Diagram
Size Varies

Purse
Project Specifications
Skill Level: Beginner
Purse Size: 13" x 8" x 3"

Note: Use a ¼" seam allowance for all steps in constructing purse.

Completing the Body of the Bag
1. Fold the 13½" x 19½" piece of fusible fleece in half across the width and crease to mark the center; place a pin on the creased line on each side.

2. Place the fleece fusible side up on the ironing board; center the A piece on the fusible fleece and press in place as shown in Figure 3. *Note: Be careful not to touch the iron directly on the fusible fleece when pressing.*

Figure 3

3. Pin and stitch a B piece to each side of A as shown in Figure 4. *Note: Sewing with a walking foot helps prevent fabric and batting from creeping during stitching.* Press B pieces to the right side onto the fusible fleece; repeat with C pieces.

Figure 4

4. Fold each E piece in half with wrong sides together to make two 4¾" x 13½" E pocket pieces.

5. Fold and crease the D piece in half across the width to mark the center of the longest side; mark a line 2½" on each side of the center crease as shown in Figure 5.

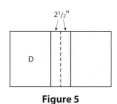

Figure 5

6. Place a folded E piece with raw edge along one marked line and folded edge toward the center of D as shown in Figure 6; stitch along the raw edge of E as shown in Figure 7; press E to the right side and pin raw edges together with D edges. Repeat with remaining E piece on the other marked line.

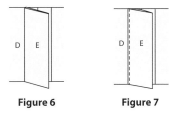

Figure 6   **Figure 7**

7. Stitch every 4½" through both D and E layers to create pocket sections as shown in Figure 8.

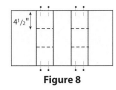

Figure 8

8. Lay the D-E unit right side down on the ironing board; center the A-B-C panel right side up on top of the D-E unit with fabric extending about 2¾" on each end as shown in Figure 9. Pin pieces together along the side edges.

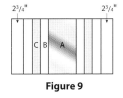

Figure 9

9. Fold each F square in half with wrong sides together on one diagonal as shown in Figure 10; press. Fold on the diagonal again and press to make a prairie point, again referring to Figure 10. Repeat to make 10 prairie points.

Figure 10

10. Arrange five prairie points along the edge of the C strip, leaving 2" at each end and overlapping prairie points as necessary to fit as shown in Figure 11; machine-baste in place to hold.

Figure 11

11. Fold each end of D under ¼" and press.

12. Hand-stitch a ⅛" button in the center of each prairie point.

Completing the Handles and Flap

1. Press under one long edge of each G strip ¼". Turn the ends of each strip under ¼" and press.

2. Lay a G strip right side down on the ironing board; center a ¾" x 20" fusible-fleece strip with fusible side down on the G strip as shown in Figure 12.

Figure 12

3. Fold the unpressed edges of G over the fleece strip and press in place. Fold the pressed edge of G over the pressed strip to cover raw edges and machine-stitch in place; stitch across each end to complete one handle; repeat steps to complete the second handle.

4. Lay an H piece right side down on the ironing board; cut one end of the 2" x 6¼" piece of fleece at a point. Center the trimmed fleece fusible side down on H and press.

5. Fold the ribbon in half to make a loop; place the loop with ends at the center of the right side of the fused H piece as shown in Figure 13; machine-baste to hold in place.

Figure 13

6. Pin the remaining H piece right sides together with the fused piece with the ribbon between; sew along sides and trimmed point of the fusible fleece to make flap, leaving the straight end open. Trim seams and turn right side out; press flat.

7. Turn the raw edges of the flap to the inside; stitch opening closed.

House of White Birches, Berne, Indiana 46711 DRGnetwork.com

Completing the Bag

1. Position the ends of the handles onto the inside of the bag body ¼" above the top of the pockets and 3" in from each side edge as shown in Figure 14; pin in place.

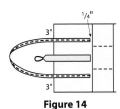

Figure 14

2. Center the flap piece on D ¼" above top of pocket, again referring to Figure 14; pin in place.

3. Fold and press the extended and pressed-under ends of D to the bag front over raw edges of the prairie points as shown in Figure 15.

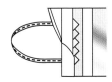

Figure 15

4. Topstitch close to the pressed edges of E to secure handles and complete the body of the bag as shown in Figure 16.

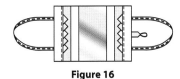

Figure 16

5. Press ends of bag body with handles and flap up and topstitch along folded edges, catching the handles and flap in the stitching as shown in Figure 17.

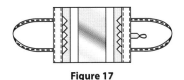

Figure 17

6. Measure, mark and stitch a line 8" down on each side of the bag body to create lines for the bag bottom as shown in Figure 18.

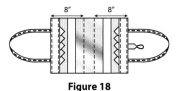

Figure 18

7. Zigzag-stitch along raw side edges of the bag body.

8. Fold the bag body in half with pockets on the outside; pin and stitch a ¼" seam allowance on both sides.

9. Fold the bottom corners up and sew a 3" seam across corner on each side to form the square corner and flat bottom of the bag as shown in Figure 19.

Figure 19

10. Turn bag right side out.

11. Fold the flap over the opposite side of the purse to close the top opening; position and stitch the button within the ribbon loop.

12. Stitch a ¼" cream button on each prairie point to finish. ❖

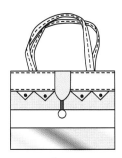

Purse
Placement Diagram 13" x 8" x 3"

Batik Beauty Patchwork Jacket

By Carol Zentgraf

Any jacket pattern can be stitched with patchwork pieces in just a few easy steps.

Project Notes

The Kwik•Sew pattern No. 3158 View B was used to make the sample jacket. It is lined without batting to make a lightweight summer jacket.

Project Specifications

Skill Level: Beginner
Jacket Size: Size varies

Materials

- ¾ yard each 3 coordinating batik prints
- 3¾ yards green print batik
- Green all-purpose thread
- Kwik•Sew pattern No. 3158
- Pattern tracing paper or tissue paper
- Basic sewing tools and supplies

Cutting Instructions

1. Cut lining and collar pieces from green print.

2. Cut front and back side panels from fabrics of choice.

Preparing the Pattern & Cutting Patchwork Pieces

Note: Use a ¼" seam allowance for all patchwork.

1. Select jacket sleeve, left front and right front pattern pieces from the commercial jacket pattern; trace each piece onto pattern tracing paper or tissue paper as shown in Figure 1. ***Note:*** *Trace half of the back pattern, flip over at the centerline and trace second half of pattern to complete tracing of the full back piece.*

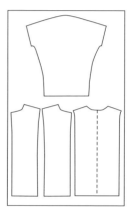

Figure 1

2. Using a straightedge and a medium-tip marker, draw horizontal and vertical lines to divide the traced pieces into gridded sections as shown in Figure 2.

Figure 2

3. Label the sections on each pattern piece with letters or numbers, again referring to Figure 2.

4. Working with one traced pattern at a time, cut out the pieces along the marked lines; arrange the pieces in order on a large flat surface.

5. Determine which pieces you want cut from each fabric; cut out, adding a ¼" seam allowance to all marked lines except the original outside lines of the pattern pieces as shown in Figure 3. ***Note:*** *The outside edges of the pattern pieces already include a ½" seam allowance. The additional ¼" seam allowance around remaining edges is used to stitch the patchwork pieces together.*

Figure 3

6. Rearrange the cut fabric pieces in order on a flat surface; sew pieces together as arranged to complete a pieced patchwork section for each pattern piece, pressing seams to one side before joining seamed sections together.

Completing the Jacket

Note: *Use a ½" seam allowance for all steps in this section.*

1. Refer to the commercial jacket-pattern instructions to assemble the jacket and lining. ***Note:*** *The sample shown was made without pockets.* ❖

Batik Beauty Patchwork Jacket Front
Placement Diagram
Size Varies

Batik Beauty Patchwork Jacket Back
Placement Diagram
Size Varies

Strip Patchwork in Black & White

By Carol Zentgraf

Combine black-and-white prints and solids to make this striking patchwork jacket.

Project Notes

Using the Kwik•Sew pattern No. 3158 View A without batting makes a lightweight summer jacket. The dolman sleeve makes it perfect for using strip-pieced patchwork strips.

Be sure to cut lining and collar pieces and the binding strips from the black-and-white print before cutting the 2" A strips.

Project Specifications

Skill Level: Beginner
Jacket Size: Size varies

Materials

- ½ yard each 2 black-with-white prints
- 1¼ yards white tonal
- 2 yards black solid
- 3½ yards black-and-white print
- White all-purpose thread
- Black and yellow 12-weight cotton thread
- ½ yard (³⁄₁₆") black twisted cord
- 4 (¾") cover buttons
- Narrow transparent tape
- Kwik•Sew pattern No. 3158
- Tissue paper
- Basic sewing tools and supplies

Cutting

1. Using the commercial pattern, cut lining and collar pieces from the black-and-white print.

2. Cut 2¼"-wide bias strips for binding to total 150" from black-and-white print. *Note: You may finish the edges of your jacket referring to the commercial pattern instructions if you prefer not to bind edges.*

3. Cut the remainder of the black-and-white print into 2" by fabric width A strips.

4. Cut the two black-with-white print fabrics into 2" by fabric width A strips.

5. Cut the white tonal into 2" by fabric width B strips.

6. Cut the black solid into 2" by fabric width C strips.

Completing the Patchwork

Note: Use a ¼" seam allowance for all patchwork and a ½" seam allowance when constructing the garment.

1. Prepare tissue-paper pattern for all jacket sections except the collar.

2. Sew an A strip to a B strip with right sides together along length; press seams toward A. Repeat with all A and B strips.

3. Join A-B strip sets to make a patchwork panel as shown in Figure 1; press seams in one direction. Repeat to make two patchwork panels. *Note: The patchwork panel length must be slightly longer than the length of the longest pattern pieces for the jacket size that you are making. The size small jacket shown used nine A-B strip sets. Add additional strip sets to the panel to make the length needed for a larger size.*

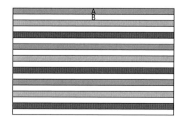

Figure 1

4. Subcut the patchwork panels into 2" A-B segments as shown in Figure 2.

Figure 2

5. Center and pin a C strip on the back tissue-paper pattern as shown in Figure 3.

Figure 3

6. Place an A-B segment right sides together with the C strip and stitch on one long edge through all layers as shown in Figure 4; press the A-B segment to the right side.

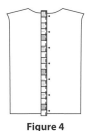

Figure 4

7. Place a C strip right sides together with the A-B segment and stitch; press C to the right side as shown in Figure 5.

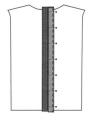

Figure 5

8. Continue to add A-B segments and C strips to cover the pattern.

9. Trim the strips even with the tissue-paper pattern edges as shown in Figure 6 to complete the back piece; remove paper pattern.

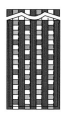

Figure 6

10. Repeat steps 5–9 to complete the remaining jacket pieces.

Completing the Jacket

Note: Use a ½" seam allowance for all steps in this section.

1. Topstitch ⅜" from seams along all C strips on the front, side and back sections using 12-weight yellow cotton thread.

2. Refer to the commercial jacket-pattern instructions to assemble the jacket and lining until the button-loop step. *Note: The sample shown does not have any pockets.*

3. Tape around the twisted cord at 3¾" intervals using narrow transparent tape; cut the cord into 4" lengths, cutting through the tape to prevent raveling.

4. Refer to the commercial jacket-pattern instructions to apply the cords for the button loops.

5. Join the 2¼"-wide bias strips on short ends to make one long strip as shown in Figure 7; press seams open.

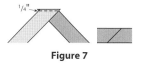

Figure 7

6. Fold the binding strip in half with wrong sides together along length; press.

7. Place the binding right sides together on the inside of the jacket, matching raw edges of binding with raw edges of jacket; stitch all around outer edges of jacket, overlapping at the beginning and end. Press binding away from jacket, and then flat along the outside edge. Machine-topstitch in place using 12-weight black cotton thread. Repeat on openings of each sleeve to complete the binding.

8. Follow manufacturer's instructions to cover buttons with black-and-white print; sew buttons to the jacket, centering on the C strips and placing them opposite loops to finish. ❖

Strip Patchwork in Black & White Back
Placement Diagram
Size Varies

Strip Patchwork in Black & White Front
Placement Diagram
Size Varies

Fleece Trapunto

When the trapunto method is used with cotton fabrics in quilts, it results in raised areas resembling embossing in the stitching or quilting design that are stuffed from the back side with batting.

When you use fleece as the fabric, the use of just two layers of fleece in the stitched design area produces the same result.

Because of the thickness of the layers, this method is most successful when stitched by machine, making it both quick and easy.

The result is a dramatic look without all the handwork required when using cotton fabrics. Refer to the instructions that follow to add a bit of class to a simple fleece jacket.

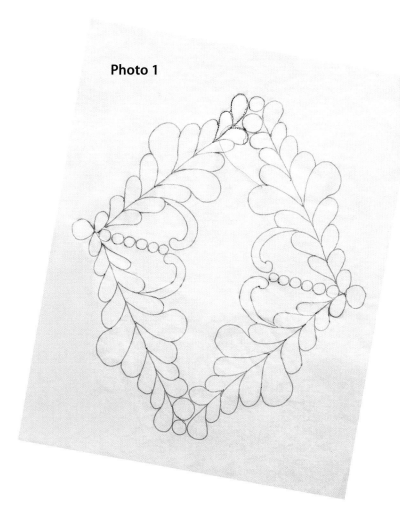

Photo 1

Materials
- Commercial jacket pattern
- Tissue paper
- Fleece as per commercial pattern, adding at least ½ yard for trapunto layer
- All-purpose thread to match fabric
- Open-toe quilting foot
- Tissue paper
- Temporary spray adhesive
- Basic sewing tools and supplies

Instructions
1. Cut a piece of fleece at least 2" larger than the design to be stitched, cutting so that the stretch of the fabric is the opposite direction of the stretch of the garment piece.

2. Transfer the chosen quilting design to tissue paper as shown in Photo 1; cut out leaving a couple of inches of paper outside the design.

3. Lightly spray the back side of the tissue-paper pattern with temporary spray adhesive.

4. Position the sprayed design on the right side of the garment in chosen location.

60

5. Lightly spray the right side of the matching-size piece of fleece with temporary spray adhesive.

6. Place the sprayed fleece against the wrong side of the garment piece behind the tissue-paper pattern and finger-press in place. *Note: Check to be sure the sprayed fleece piece stretches in the opposite direction as the garment piece and that all areas of the paper design have the piece of fleece behind them; there will be three layers to stitch through. It is difficult to tell the right and wrong side of some fleece. If this is the case, there is no need to worry about right and wrong sides.*

Photo 2

7. Using matching all-purpose thread in the top of the machine and an open-toe quilting foot, sew over the lines on the tissue paper.

8. Using sharp scissors, cut off excess fleece from around the outside edge and in any large open areas of the design on the fleece piece on the inside of the garment as shown in Photo 2, being careful not to clip through the garment.

9. Stitching through the bulky layers of the fleece results in a decorative raised design as shown in Photo 3. ❖

Photo 3

62

Special Thanks

Please join us in thanking the talented designers listed below for their work.

Bren Bornyasz
Stack & Cut Squares Jacket, 30
Stitch & Flip Jacket, 10

Colleen Granger
Abstract Jacket, 16

Connie Kauffman
Feathered Fleece Jacket, 36
Jelly Jacket & Purse, 42

Chris Malone
Denim & Floral Duo, 22

Lorine Mason
Flowers & Vines Sweatshirt Jacket, 4

Carol Zentgraf
Batik Beauty Patchwork Jacket, 50
Strip Patchwork in Black & White, 54

Fabric & Supplies

Page 10, Stitch & Flip Jacket—
The Mount Fuji Jacket from Brensan Studios.

Page 30, Stack & Cut Squares Jacket—
The Quarter Circle Jacket BSS111 from Brensan Studios.

Page 36, Feathered Fleece Jacket—
KK2000 Temporary Spray Adhesive, Blendable cotton thread and Tender Touch and Soft-and-Sheer stabilizers from Sulky of America.

Page 42, Jelly Jacket & Purse—
Simplicity fabric collection from Moda, cotton and Blendable threads from Sulky of America and Fusible Warm Fleece from The Warm Co.

Page 50, Batik Beauty Patchwork Jacket—
Artisan Batik fabrics from Robert Kaufman.

Page 54, Strip Patchwork in Black & White—
Black twisted cord No.IR2349BK from Expo International, www.expointl.com; cover buttons from Prym Consumer USA, www.prymdritz.com; Kona fabrics from Robert Kaufman, www.robertkaufman.com; 12-weight cotton thread from Sulky of America, www.sulky.com; and Kwik•Sew pattern 3158, View A, www.kwiksew.com.

Easy Patchwork Jackets

Metric Conversion Charts

Metric Conversions

Canada/U.S. Measurement		Multiplied by		Metric Measurement
yards	x	.9144	=	metres (m)
yards	x	91.44	=	centimetres (cm)
inches	x	2.54	=	centimetres (cm)
inches	x	25.40	=	millimetres (mm)
inches	x	.0254	=	metres (m)

Metric Measurement		Multiplied by		Canada/U.S. Measurement
centimetres	x	.3937	=	inches
metres	x	1.0936	=	yards

Standard Equivalents

Canada/U.S. Measurement		Metric Measurement		
⅛ inch	=	3.20 mm	=	0.32 cm
¼ inch	=	6.35 mm	=	0.635 cm
⅜ inch	=	9.50 mm	=	0.95 cm
½ inch	=	12.70 mm	=	1.27 cm
⅝ inch	=	15.90 mm	=	1.59 cm
¾ inch	=	19.10 mm	=	1.91 cm
⅞ inch	=	22.20 mm	=	2.22 cm
1 inch	=	25.40 mm	=	2.54 cm
⅛ yard	=	11.43 cm	=	0.11 m
¼ yard	=	22.86 cm	=	0.23 m
⅜ yard	=	34.29 cm	=	0.34 m
½ yard	=	45.72 cm	=	0.46 m
⅝ yard	=	57.15 cm	=	0.57 m
¾ yard	=	68.58 cm	=	0.69 m
⅞ yard	=	80.00 cm	=	0.80 m
1 yard	=	91.44 cm	=	0.91 m

Canada/U.S. Measurement		Metric Measurement		
1⅛ yard	=	102.87 cm	=	1.03 m
1¼ yard	=	114.30 cm	=	1.14 m
1⅜ yard	=	125.73 cm	=	1.26 m
1½ yard	=	137.16 cm	=	1.37 m
1⅝ yard	=	148.59 cm	=	1.49 m
1¾ yard	=	160.02 cm	=	1.60 m
1⅞ yard	=	171.44 cm	=	1.71 m
2 yards	=	182.88 cm	=	1.83 m
2⅛ yards	=	194.31 cm	=	1.94 m
2¼ yards	=	205.74 cm	=	2.06 m
2⅜ yards	=	217.17 cm	=	2.17 m
2½ yards	=	228.60 cm	=	2.29 m
2⅝ yards	=	240.03 cm	=	2.40 m
2¾ yards	=	251.46 cm	=	2.51 m
2⅞ yards	=	262.88 cm	=	2.63 m
3 yards	=	274.32 cm	=	2.74 m
3⅛ yards	=	285.75 cm	=	2.86 m
3¼ yards	=	297.18 cm	=	2.97 m
3⅜ yards	=	308.61 cm	=	3.09 m
3½ yards	=	320.04 cm	=	3.20 m
3⅝ yards	=	331.47 cm	=	3.31 m
3¾ yards	=	342.90 cm	=	3.43 m
3⅞ yards	=	354.32 cm	=	3.54 m
4 yards	=	365.76 cm	=	3.66 m
4⅛ yards	=	377.19 cm	=	3.77 m
4¼ yards	=	388.62 cm	=	3.89 m
4⅜ yards	=	400.05 cm	=	4.00 m
4½ yards	=	411.48 cm	=	4.11 m
4⅝ yards	=	422.91 cm	=	4.23 m
4¾ yards	=	434.34 cm	=	4.34 m
4⅞ yards	=	445.76 cm	=	4.46 m
5 yards	=	457.20 cm	=	4.57 m

E-mail: Customer_Service@whitebirches.com

HOUSE of WHITE BIRCHES
PUBLISHERS SINCE 1947

Easy Patchwork Jackets is published by DRG, 306 East Parr Road, Berne, IN 46711, telephone (260) 589-4000. Printed in USA. Copyright © 2009 DRG. All rights reserved. This publication may not be reproduced in part or in whole without written permission from the publisher.

RETAIL STORES: If you would like to carry this pattern book or any other DRG publications, call the Wholesale Department at Annie's Attic to set up a direct account: (903) 636-4303. Also, request a complete listing of publications available from DRG.

Every effort has been made to ensure that the instructions in this pattern book are complete and accurate. We cannot, however, take responsibility for human error, typographical mistakes or variations in individual work.

STAFF

Editor: Jeanne Stauffer, Sandra L. Hatch
Managing Editor: Dianne Schmidt
Technical Artist: Connie Rand
Copy Supervisor: Michelle Beck
Copy Editor: Amanda Ladig, Renee Wright
Graphic Arts Supervisor: Ronda Bechinski

Graphic Artists: Pam Gregory, Erin Augsburger
Art Director: Brad Snow
Assistant Art Director: Nick Pierce
Photography Supervisor: Tammy Christian
Photography: Scott Campbell
Photo Stylist: Martha Coquat

ISBN: 978-1-59217-238-2
1 2 3 4 5 6 7 8 9

House of White Birches, Berne, Indiana 46711   DRGnetwork.com

Photo Index

22

16

4

10

50

36

30

54

42

59